Louis Jackson, T. S Brown

Our Caughnawagas in Egypt

Louis Jackson, T. S Brown

Our Caughnawagas in Egypt

ISBN/EAN: 9783742873385

Manufactured in Europe, USA, Canada, Australia, Japa

Cover: Foto ©Andreas Hilbeck / pixelio.de

Manufactured and distributed by brebook publishing software
(www.brebook.com)

Louis Jackson, T. S Brown

Our Caughnawagas in Egypt

A Narrative of what was seen and accomplished by the Contingent of North American Indian Voyageurs who led the British Boat Expedition for the Relief of Khartoum up the Cataracts of the Nile.

By LOUIS JACKSON, of Caughnawaga,
Captain of the Contingent.   ·

With an introductory preface by C. S. Brown.

Montreal :
W. DRYSDALE & CO.,
PUBLISHERS, BOOKSELLERS AND STATIONERS,
232 St. James Street.

1885.

PREFACE.

———o———

THE Indians of Caughnawaga are an offshoot from the Mohawks, one of the divisions of the Six Nations, formerly in pseudo occupation of western New York, and known to the French by the general name of Iroquois. Long before the cession of this Province to Great Britain, they were settled at the head of the rapids of the St. Lawrence opposite Lachine, on a tract of land ten miles square, or 64,000 acres held in common, but lately separated into lots to be divided among the people as individual property.

Contrary to what has been the too common fate of aborigines brought into close contact with foreigners, the Caughnawagas, with some mixture of white blood, have maintained throughout, their Indian customs, manners and language, with the manhood of their ancestors, in an alertness, strength and power of endurance wherever these qualities have been required : in the boating or rafting on our larger rivers and the hardships of *Voyageurs* in the North-West.

As a high tribute to this known excellence, the call for Canadian *Voyageurs* to assist in the boat navigation of the Nile was accompanied by a special requirement that there should be a contingent of fifty Caughnawagas. They responded quickly to the call, performed the task committed to them in a manner most satisfactory as described in these pages, and returned to their homes at the end of six months, after a voyage of more than 12,000 miles, sound and resolute as when they started, with the loss of but two men.

There is something unique in the idea of the aborigines of the New World being sent for to teach the Egyptians how to pass the Cataracts of the Nile, which has been navigated in some way by them for thousands of years, that should make this little book attractive to all readers, especially as it is written by one born and bred in Caughnawaga, who, with the quick eye of an Indian, has noticed many things unnoticed by ordinary tourists and travellers.

It is written in a most excellent spirit that might wisely be imitated by other travellers. The writer finds no faults, blames nobody, and always content, is generous in his acknowledgments for every act of kindness and proper consideration shown to him and his party, by Her Majesty's Officers of all ranks in command of the expedition. It was written off-hand and goes forth to the public as it came from the pen of the writer, to be judged in its style and the matter contained, by no standard but its own.

MONTREAL, April, 1885.

OUR CAUGHNAWAGAS IN EGYPT.

When it was made known by Lord Melgund in the early part of September, 1884, that it was the express desire of General Lord Wolseley to have Caughnawaga Indians form part of the Canadian Contingent, the required number was soon obtained, in spite of discouraging talk and groundless fears. Having been introduced to Lord Melgund, I agreed to go and look after the Caughnawaga boys, although then busily engaged in securing my crops. I, with a number of others reached the "Ocean King" at Quebec, having been left behind in Montreal through incorrect information given me by one of the ship's officers as to the time of sailing. We received the farewell of the Governor General on board the "Ocean King," and His Excellency's very kind words had an especially encouraging effect upon my boys.

On reaching Sidney, C. B., and while taking in coal, some funny tricks were played by voyageurs which I must not omit. To get ashore in spite of the officers who kept watch on the wharf, some daring fellows jumped from the vessel's rigging into the empty coal cars returning to the wharf, coming back in the dark and the vessel being a few feet off the wharf, the men had to climb aboard by a rope. Now it happened, that of two friends, one was able to get up, the other was not, neither could his friend help him, they however, contrived a plan, which they

carried out to perfection. The one on the wharf laid
quietly down, while his friend climbed aboard and
there informed our officers that a man had hurt himself by falling off the coal shoot, immediately there
was great alarm, lamps were hung over the side and
the man discovered by his clothes to be one of the
voyageurs, a plank was shoved out over the ship's
rail, standing nearly upright and a line hove, (some
suggested to put the line around his neck.) However,
he was hoisted aboard and carried towards the cabin.
While being carried, the apparently lifeless one was
seen to open his eyes three or four times, but too
many hands evidently had hold of him and so he was
brought before the doctor, who eagerly examined
him, but soon pronounced him dead, " dead drunk " and
ordered him to be taken to his bunk, where he soon
sat up laughing and feeling good, to escape so easily.

On arriving in Alexandria, after a fine passage and
good treatment we saw our boats, which at the first
sight and from a distance, were condemned by the
boys, but later experience changed our first impression.

We left the wharf at Alexandria on the 8th of October, at 11 a. m. by train. The first-class carriages
were after the English style, but the troop cars in
which we were transported were less comfortable,
they had four benches placed fore and aft, two in the
centre back to back and one on each side with back to
outside, lacking the usual conveniences of our Canadian
cars. The sides of the car were about four feet
high, then open to the roof. We were fifty-
six in a car which made it uncomfortably crowded.
After leaving Alexandria I was surprised to see

people standing up to their necks in the swamps, cutting some kind of grass. I saw also cattle lying perfectly still in the water with just their heads out. This sight scared my boys as to what the heat would be further south. Beyond the swamps on the east side of the road I saw nice gardens, and, what was still more interesting, groves of palm trees with fruit After two hours' ride we reached the desert, where nothing but sand was to be seen. The whistle went all the time to warn camel drivers, who also use the roadbed, and I did not see any other road for them to travel. Another curiosity was the protective fencing for the road, made of cornstalks to keep back the sand, as we make board fences against the snow. At all the stations, which were far apart, all hands rushed out for a drink of water. We did not meet many trains. During the afternoon we came close to the Nile, which there appeared to be about the same width as the St. Lawrence opposite Caughnawaga. We soon reached a regular Egyptian settlement, with people living in small mud huts, and with chickens, goats, sheep and dogs coming out with the children. The ground appeared to be clay and in the road every three or four feet there was a rat hole and rats dodging in all directions. I saw more rats at a glance than I had ever seen before in all my life. We also saw some ship yards with some boats on the stocks and some on the mud. The boats were about twenty feet long, and one afloat appeared to be wood to within about four inches above water with gunwales of mud and a peculiar sail.

The gunwales were three or four feet high and

five or six inches thick. They appeared to be baked
hard by the sun, and were water proof, as I afterwards
saw several of them loaded so heavily that a great
part of the mud gunwales were under water. I sup-
pose mud is used in preference to wood, because wood
is very scarce in Egypt and mud is very plentiful.
They make the most of the mud which the Nile
brings down in such quantities every year. They
build houses with it as well as boats and it is this
mud which manures and fertilizes the whole land of
Egypt.

We soon sighted the pyramids and came to Bulac
Station three miles from Cairo at 7 o'clock. It being
dark, supper was served which we took into the cars,
it consisted of canned meat, bread and tea. We left at
eight for Assiout. The sand became very trouble-
some entering the open cars and I concluded as we
were travelling through the night to give my eyes a
rest and went to sleep sitting up. Next morning at
eight o'clock we reached Assiout about 240 miles
from Alexandria, there we saw some Nubian prisoners,
black, ugly and desperate looking fellows chained
together with large rusty chains round their necks.
They were sitting on the ground. We were marched
about a quarter of a mile to the river, where there
were fleets of steamers and barges, one fleet waiting
for us. We were marched on board two barges tied
together and after washing about half an inch of mud
off our faces with Nile river water, went to breakfast
prepared by our own cooks who had left Alexandria
twelve hours in advance. After breakfast I went
ashore, I noticed in one little mud hut, goats, sheep,

THE PYRAMIDS OF GHIZEH.

THE GREAT SPHINX.

dogs and children on the ground and there were flies in the children's faces and eyes beyond description. I got my first near view of a date tree here with its rough bark which I cut with my knife.

The next sight was a ship yard where four or five whip saws were kept going; their whip saw is rigged like a bucksaw only the saw instead of the stick, is in the centre. There is a stick on each side of the saw and a string outside each stick. They had to back the saw the whole length of the wood to get it out. Messrs. Cook and Son the great tourist agents had just commenced to build a large hotel, which when returning home I found already finished. I noticed a sign over a mud house door " Egyptian Bank." A track runs from the depot straight down to the river and there were a number of flat cars loaded with boats, of which I took a nearer look, I also saw oars and poles. I was well pleased with all and at the same time made up my mind, that we had carried paddles across the ocean for very little use. I asked permission to go and see the catacombs, but was told that we must get under way. I received for my men cooking utensils, such as kettles, tin-plates, knives, forks and spoons, for the whole campaign, which I delivered up again, when returning. We started at 11 a. m., the fleet consisting of two barges side by side in tow of a side-wheel steamer. At the stern of each barge a trough, built of mud bricks, formed the cooking range, and it amused me to see that they had put on about half a cord of wood for cooking purposes, to last during the trip to Assouan, (twelve days) and this at once impressed me with the difference between the value of fuel in this country and in our own. There were thirteen gangs with their foremen on the barges and three gangs with foremen on the steamer. We found the Nile river water of good taste but muddy and we generally left it standing for an hour to settle. A funny sight was presented by a cow and a small camel harnessed to a plough. A stick crooked suitably by nature was laid over both necks and tied round each and a native rope was run from the yoke to a stick, also crooked to suit the purpose by nature, used as plough, scratching about two inches deep and three inches wide, at a speed as I judged of one acre per week. Another unusual thing was to see the crops in several stages of growth at the same time in adjoining patches, from sowing to quarter grown half grown and ripe crops. This is one of the consequences of the Nubians depending upon the overflow of the Nile to fertilize their soil. Directly the river begins to fall they commence to sow their seed in the mud, it leaves behind, and as the water recedes they follow it up with the sowing. The crop farthest from the river of course gets the start.

The next novel sight was the irrigation of the fields. To lift the water from the river, a frame is made by putting some cornstalks into the ground and putting clay round them to make posts, which are placed about six feet apart; the posts support a small stick, across which is laid a crooked pole, with about a dozen bends in it, that balances a mud basket on one end against a leather bucket on the other. The bucket holds about as much as our common well bucket. a man is continually filling from the river and empty-

dogs and children on the ground and there were flies in the children's faces and eyes beyond description. I got my first near view of a date tree here with its rough bark which I cut with my knife.

The next sight was a ship yard where four or five whip saws were kept going; their whip saw is rigged like a bucksaw only the saw instead of the stick, is in the centre. There is a stick on each side of the saw and a string outside each stick. They had to back the saw the whole length of the wood to get it out. Messrs. Cook and Son the great tourist agents had just commenced to build a large hotel, which when returning home I found already finished. I noticed a sign over a mud house door " Egyptian Bank." A track runs from the depot straight down to the river and there were a number of flat cars loaded with boats, of which I took a nearer look, I also saw oars and poles. I was well pleased with all and at the same time made up my mind, that we had carried paddles across the ocean for very little use. I asked permission to go and see the catacombs, but was told that we must get under way. I received for my men cooking utensils, such as kettles, tin-plates, knives, forks and spoons, for the whole campaign, which I delivered up again, when returning. We started at 11 a. m., the fleet consisting of two barges side by side in tow of a side-wheel steamer. At the stern of each barge a trough, built of mud bricks, formed the cooking range, and it amused me to see that they had put on about half a cord of wood for cooking purposes, to last during the trip to Assouan, (twelve days) and this at once impressed me with the difference between the value of fuel in this country and in our own. There were thirteen gangs with their foremen on the barges and three gangs with foremen on the steamer. We found the Nile river water of good taste but muddy and we generally left it standing for an hour to settle. A funny sight was presented by a cow and a small camel harnessed to a plough. A stick crooked suitably by nature was laid over both necks and tied round each and a native rope was run from the yoke to a stick, also crooked to suit the purpose by nature, used as plough, scratching about two inches deep and three inches wide, at a speed as I judged of one acre per week. Another unusual thing was to see the crops in several stages of growth at the same time in adjoining patches, from sowing to quarter grown half grown and ripe crops. This is one of the consequences of the Nubians depending upon the overflow of the Nile to fertilize their soil. Directly the river begins to fall they commence to sow their seed in the mud, it leaves behind, and as the water recedes they follow it up with the sowing. The crop farthest from the river of course gets the start.

The next novel sight was the irrigation of the fields. To lift the water from the river, a frame is made by putting some cornstalks into the ground and putting clay round them to make posts, which are placed about six feet apart; the posts support a small stick, across which is laid a crooked pole, with about a dozen bends in it, that balances a mud basket on one end against a leather bucket on the other. The bucket holds about as much as our common well bucket. a man is continually filling from the river and empty-

A DAHABEAH.

RAISING WATER ON THE NILE.

ing into a mud spout between the posts. The water
is led off in a small mud conduit over the farm which
is divided into sections, when one section is filled
with water the stream is turned into another one.
These waterworks are kept going day and night. Once
in a while one may see cattle power used for irrigation of the following old fashioned kind, the yoke is
hitched to a primative cog-wheel of about twelve feet
in diameter, which works into a smaller wheel placed
underneath it, the cattle walking over a bridge. The
cogs are simply pins driven into the outside of each
wheel. The shaft of the smaller wheel runs out over
a ditch cut from the river and carries a large reel
about eighteen feet in diameter over which two native
ropes are laid to which are attached about forty earth-
en jars. The cattle here are about the same size as
ours, but they have a lump on their back and their
horns run straight back. The colour of most of these
cattle is blueish. Where the fertile strip of land
is wide, canals are dug in curves to bring
the water back near, to the sand mountains. The
cattle feed along the river bank, which is left uncul-
tivated for about twenty feet from the water, and I
have seen a number of them of all kinds, feeding on
this poor strip and never touch the rich crops along-
side, although left to themselves and I was told that
they were taught that way. The sheep look
like dogs dragging long tails on the ground and the
dogs look much like the Esquimaux dogs I have seen
in Manitoba.

After seven or eight days travel we left the sand
mountains and began to see rock on both sides, more

particularly on the east bank the rock looked to me
like plaster of Paris. The natives quarried it and
loaded it into small dibeers. "Dibeers" are sailing
crafts with a small cabin aft, whilst, "Nuggars" are
plain barges, with a very peculiar sail, the boom of
which is rolled into the sail by way of furling the latter. I heard one blast go off and this being Sunday,
the 19th October, I made up my mind that the people
here have no Sundays. We passed some ruins on both
shores, some appeared to be cut into the solid rock,
which here is of a brownish colour. I could not tell
what kind of rock but the courses varied from four to
twenty feet as seen between the temples and they
laid very even The perpendicular seams were perfectly straight. The temples all faced the river. We
also passed some immense figures, some standing, some
sitting on chairs, some looking towards the river,
some showing their profile, the highest of these I
judged to be 60 feet high. It was a pity that we
could not get the slightest information from the
Egyptian crew with us, who seemed very averse to
us, so much so, that I could not even learn their names
far less any of their language. About this time some
of the boys gave out that we would be shown the
exact spot, where Moses was picked up, but nobody
knew exactly. Our fleet did not run at nights, and it
always happened that we halted in some uninhabited
place, where nothing could be learned. Some of the
cities we passed presented a beautiful appearance
from the distance, temples, high towers and so forth
all looking very white, some mud houses were two
or three stories high and of blue mud color.

At one place, the only one point where we stopped in the day time, I went ashore to see what was called a sacred tree. A young Christian Egyptian of about sixteen years, whose acquaintance I made here told me that the sacred tree had great healing power, and sick people would come and ask its help, and when cured would drive a nail into the tree as a memorial. The tree showed a great number of nails of all patterns, and it must not be forgotten that nails here are even scarcer than money. It is a live tree and nothing nice to look at, it rises from the ground about four feet straight and then lays over horizontally for about thirty feet, after which it turns up and throws out branches. The trunk is about one foot through and the bark is similar to that of our large thorn tree. Returning to the fleet I saw a young man lying in the dust on the side of the road, with his mouth open, his tongue out and his eyes, in fact his whole face a mass of flies, a horrible sight. A little girl bent over him, pointed to the sick and looked at me. My young Christian bade me come away saying it was a case of leprosy. My friend showed me a mosque and a bazaar. Coming out of the bazaar I noticed three men acting very queerly, walking around in front of a mud hut, talking dolefully or murmuring and constantly looking to the ground, and was told that there was a death in the family. My guide saw me back to the fleet and on the road asked me for a book, and I gave him one. His people lived in the place. The fertile strips along the river here are much narrower than in Lower Egypt, sometimes one-eighth of a mile wide sometimes only about two hundred feet, but to judge from the crops as well as the cattle and the food the latter find, the soil must be better.

I should say the river is from a third of a mile to half a mile wide on the average from Assiout to Assouan, and very shallow, as the steamer, which drew about five feet of water, got aground often. We reached Assouan at 10 a. m. on the 21st, not without regret at having had to pass such famous places as Thebes and Luxor. We camped quite close to Thebes and there were guides waiting with candles to show us over the place but we had no time to spare and so were not permitted to wander about.

We landed two miles below the city at Assouan the lower end of the track of the seven mile railway to Shellal passing behind Assouan. This railway is built to portage over the first cataract. Opposite Assouan, we passed the camp of the Black Watch. At Shellal, a steamer with forty whalers in tow received us and started at once towards Wady Halfa. We camped two or three miles above Shellal and were therefore deprived of any sight of the first cataract. Our fifty-six Caughnawaga Indians were given eight boats, which were towed four abreast and ten long, this was the first time we got into the boats. We soon made use of the awning provided for each. The country along the river here is all rock and as I was told, back of the rock all sand. Doctor Neilson informed me that we were now about crossing into the tropics. The natives here are considerably darker than the Egyptians and better built men. They were dressed similarly to the Egyptians. A navy pinnace over-hauled us here bringing Abbe Bouchard who had

stayed behind in Cairo. We went a good distance
before we again met cultivated land and then only in
strips, some of which were not twenty feet wide and
they were utilized every inch. The natives follow
the falling river with cultivation, as I discovered when
coming back a little over three months afterwards,
when I found crops of beans from one inch to a foot
long, growing where there had been water. We
passed miles of barren rock and then again narrow strips and altogether the country was poorer
than Upper Egypt. Occasionally we would see a
few date trees along the river and now and then
a small mud-built village. Irrigation was going on
the same as below, both by hand and by
ox-power. We reached Korosko on the 24th of October the steamer was run with the bow on the shore, but
the boats towed too far from shore for us to get out.

Korosko is a small fort occupied by both English
and Egyptian soldiers The river banks around
are fifteen to twenty feet high. From my whaler
I could see a small building near the beach
with a sign over the door marked " poste Keden "
Post office. We left Korosko after an hour's stoppage
and beached in good season, to give us a chance to
cook supper. At every night's camp we unavoidably
did more or less damage to the crops, which must have
caused serious loss to these poor people by whom, as I
said before, every inch of the spare soil is utilized.
We got under way at sunrise. The river up this far
from Assouan is a series of very straight stretches from
five to fifteen miles in length with no difficult bends
and good for navigation everywhere. The current

varys from three to five miles an hour. During this day I noticed a small screw tug bearing a foresail coming after us and trying hard to reach us It proved to be a press steamer having on board the correspondent of an English paper, an engineer and a native pilot. They ran short of coal and wanted a tow, and all the coal they had left when reaching us, a man could have put in his vest pocket We beached this night on the west side close to a temple, cut, as it appeared to me into the solid rock. Being called to receive stores and cholera belts for the men I was prevented from joining an exploring party, that set out, and was told, when the boys came back, that I had missed something worth seeing. I learnt afterwards that this place was Abu-Simbel, where there are two temples cut out of the rock which are said to be the oldest specimens of architecture in the world. The boys said they had seen stone figures of men with toes three feet long and I dare say they were not far out, as I learnt there are four seated figures in front of the largest temple supposed to represent Rameses the Great, which are sixty five feet in height. I was sorry that I had to stay behind to look after the stores, Talking about cholera belts, everybody engaged in the British service in Egypt had to wear these belts, soldiers and voyageurs were supplied with them and required to wear them. They are strips of flannel twelve or fifteen inches wide, and I was told by soldiers who had served in Egypt some time, that they are very effective in preventing cholera and dysentery.

Next day, Sunday the 26th at 5 p. m. we arrived at

Wady Halfa. The weather was still the same as ever since we landed at Alexandria, not a cloud, not uncomfortably warm, but warm enough. A steam tug came out from Wady Halfa and brought orders for us to proceed as far as the river was navigable for the steamer. This brought us about four miles above Wady Halfa where the tow was disbanded. The boats then proceeded another mile and we camped. During this mile we had the first opportunity to work the boats, (still all light) and that evening the opinions about them varied greatly.

No sooner were our tents pitched than Lord Wolseley arrived. He shook hands with some, exchanged a few words with our commander, Colonel Denison, and was off again. We found here about a hundred whalers waiting for us. We were at the foot of the second cataract and the following morning were ordered to take the light boats up the cataract to the first naval camp, about three miles distant, to make one trip and if possible two. Seven men took one boat and all the crews made two trips, some getting through early, some late.

The first trip I made, I took a different channel from those who started before. I stepped the two masts with which the boat was provided and used the sails and the six oars only, the wind being as usual from the north. We needed all our resources but we reached the camp in good time. We walked back the three miles took another boat and tried the channel generally taken, it being apparently the shortest route I had to use the tow-line at one place where there was a "gate" or channel, as we say in Canada, with about

three feet of a fall, about eighteen feet wide and a good
standing place to tow from. Right there was stationed
our acquaintance, the reporter, in his little tug moored
above the gate. One of the voyageurs while wading
must have stepped into some seam, he jumped quickly
back into his boat, leaving behind his moccasin and
said he was bitten by a crocodile, which all of us were
kind enough to believe and we advised him not to wade
any more. All had accomplished their task in the evening and come back to our camp. Soon afterwards General Sir Evelyn Wood arrived and went towards
Colonel Denison's tent. I heard my name called by
my officer and went before the General who demanded
the number of my men and wanted to see them.
Getting the men in line, the General asked me if they
spoke English and I said they spoke enough for boating
purposes, but no more. The General then left. After
supper I was informed by my officer that I had to
take thirty-five men with me and go about a hundred
miles up the river.

Here commences the second railway of the river route,
about thirty miles long. and the first train on the following morning brought Lord Wolseley on his way to
the front. The second train had on board, Col.
Alleyne, Lord Avonmore, Capt. Moore, Lieut. Perry
and Lieut. C. R. Orde. This train took me and my
men on and stopped at Gemai where we found several
boats which had been portaged on cars. We pitched
tents and did not leave until 10 o'clock the next morning, October 29th. I picked crews as nearly equal
as I could, with a captain to each and started with six
boats, nearly light, only the five officers and their lugg-

BOAT FOR THE NILE EXPEDITION UNDER SAIL.

BOAT FOR THE NILE EXPEDITION SHOWING AWNING.

age on board. I had the honor to start in boat No. 1 with Col. Alleyne on board, the officers taking a boat each of different numbers, reached Sarras about 5 p. m. a distance of eighteen miles. The river here is very narrow, in some places about a thousand feet and the current very swift. I had to get a line out only once. At Sarras each boat took on nearly two tons of ammunition and stores, also additional passengers. We proceeded two miles up and camped. There were many islands and rocks both in sight and sunken, but room enough to go anywhere. The shores are barren rock. Starting next day with a light breeze, I soon found that I wanted more wind to proceed under sail as the current grew swifter and my boat had now on board, besides Col. Alleyne, his servant, his interpreter one corporal and one native swimmer, then myself with five men and about two tons of freight. This was the time to find out what we could do with our boats, the northwind had freshened, which gave us more speed and with the help of five good oars we dodged the swift currents, catching eddies and after two hours trial the captains congratulated each other upon being masters of the situation. We soon began to race each captain using his own judgment as to which channel to take, which gave each a chance to be ahead or behind according to his luck. When I signalled for dinner all headed for shore and it was here that Louis Capitaine was so unaccountably lost, within sixty feet from shore. Louis had the bow oar in Peter January's boat and he rose when nearing shore. While standing in the bow he fell over, the headway of the boat made the distance a hundred

feet before he was seen to rise. Lieut. Perry threw a
life-preserver and ordered the Arab swimmer, which
this boat carried, to assist him, the swimmer jumped
immediately and swam towards the spot but Louis
disappeared before assistance reached him. My
boat was about sixty yards behind Peter's boat
coming up in the eddy behind a rock. When striking
the current I noticed Louis' helmet and the Arab
swimmer. We went ashore to prepare dinner and I
really believe that Colonel Alleyne, the officer in
charge of this convoy, felt so badly about this accident,
that he did not take anything. He hired natives to
search for the body and give it decent burial, if found.
After dinner we proceeded with one man short. The
water not being so bad we made the Semnah cataract
that afternoon. This cataract was thought the worst
in the whole route. Colonel Alleyne showed me up to
the gate and said " now everything is yours." It
must be understood that this gate does by no means
reach across the river. The river is about 1000 feet
wide here and the gate situated between the east
shore and an island is about twenty feet wide. Not
being sure of the water I tried a light boat first. I
took boat No. 1 through without any trouble, but
would not trust the full load on any boat. We all
lightened somewhat and passed the six boats through
with tow lines inside of an hour. The freight we
had left was portaged by camels. We reloaded and
started under sail four miles up in smooth water and
camped. Colonel Alleyne held an inquest that night
on Louis Capitaine's death and despatched a man to the
nearest telegraph station with the news of his death.

CATARACT OF AMBIGOL.

A few weeks after this despatch was sent, Colonel
Kennedy showed me a copy of the Ottawa *Free Press*,
in which the *Free Press* made free indeed reporting
Captain Louis Jackson as drowned. All the captains
appeared pleased with their boats, talking about who
made the best run and each boasting to have the best
boat From this cataract to the next one above, at
Ambigol, is counted seventeen miles, which stretch
proved much the same as below Semnah cataract;
plenty of dodging and crossing the stream to get the
side of the river with the lesser current, the boats
being such good travellers and answering their helms
so well with a stiff breeze, we found ourselves in a
genuine boatman's paradise. In spite of the free wind
we had all day, we had to get lines out and track
several times. We camped on an island about a
mile below Ambigol cataract In the evening the
captains argued as to which of them had run the
most on sandbanks. These sand shoals are formed
behind large rocks in a manner never seen in our
own waters, and it was strange to notice that like
situated rocks would not alike accumulate sand, some
had shoals behind them and some had none, still all
showed the same eddy on the water surface, and the
water being muddy we could not tell which to trust
and so gave them all wider berths in future.

The following day, the 1st of November we reached
the post of Ambigol about 8 a. m. We found this
cataract different from Semnah cataract. This has no
" gate " but a very crooked channel, swift current and
very bad tracking. It required the combined force of
thirty-five men to pull one boat with its full load.

The cataract is one mile long and the roughest part is at the foot and at the head. It was in this mile of the route that afterwards three white men were lost. We got through this cataract about noon and cooked dinner just above it. It must be remembered that the route was entirely unknown to us all and that we had to find our channels and often did not take the best one. From this out I ordered my captains to take a different channel each, there being so many, so as to find the best one for future purposes. The boats being so equally matched, we could easily tell who had the wrong channel, for he was soon left astern. The officer in charge, Col. Alleyne, who is himself an experienced boatman, was so well pleased with our progress that he never interfered but left it all to us. It must also not be forgotten that the boys had been forty days travelling, doing no hard work, before we took the boats and by this time their hands were very sore. The rocky shores were so bold that poles could only be of use in keeping off and it was impossible to assist by shoving ahead.

To say a word about the boats now, we all had come to the conclusion that the boats and outfit were well devised for the service so far. We had tried them now in various ways; we had sailed against a swift current with a beam wind, where a flat bottom would have had to be towed with lines, and the more this towing could be avoided the better it was on account of the fearful track along the shore. The boats. were sufficiently strong for all necessary handling and in case of accident, they were light enough to be brought ashore and turned over for repairs without extra help. More difficult it was to find a good place on the shore where to haul a boat out. The boats were provided with two sails each, a sample of which (sails) I have brought home with me.

We camped next on Tangur island and the following day the 2nd of November, we started to face the Tangur cataract. The wind being very strong in our favor we tried to dodge behind the many islands, but had to give up sailing in many places and get the lines out. We overcame this cataract without much difficulty. Above the cataract it was considered smooth water for about one mile when a very bad stretch was met with about half a mile long. The river here is about quarter of a mile wide, and full of large rocks between which the water came down very "wicked" in channels of about sixty feet wide and some wider. I again ordered each captain to pick his own channel, and having a strong breeze and all oars working we managed to get above. In this place I discovered by experience that what we had found to be the best channel on that day, was the worst a few days after. The water falling six inches to a foot every day, continually changed the rapids, making a bad place better and a good place bad. Above this cataract we had thirteen miles of what we called smooth water with a current of from three to five miles an hour. I had noticed in coming up that the country was inhabited, having seen a few Arabs now and then. We reached the foot of Akaska cataract that evening. On landing, the boat, which carried Lord Avonmore, got stove in when His Lordship took the tools and proved himself quite a carpenter. Here also were seen some useful stretches of beach under cultivation, but these were getting few and far between.

Next day. the 3rd November, we faced the Akaska cataract, we were getting used to the river and therefore this cataract proved to be the easiest so far. Between Akaska and the foot of Dal cataract there are nine miles of good navigation, and the greater part of the beach is useful, this stretch looking altogether better and less wild. We reached the foot of Dal about noon. Dal cataract is said to be five miles long In this cataract I saw for the first time, small willow trees on the islands. We went about half a mile up with sails and oars, when we had to track for quite a distance. In this rapid it happened for the first time that we came to a halt, not knowing how to proceed. We had crossed on to an island not having water enough in the little channel between this island and the shore, but found at the head of the island the water rough and the current too strong to pull against and could not proceed without a line to the mainshore. It was here that the foresight of Colonel Alleyne, proved of value. Our Arab swimmer managed to carry the tow line to the shore, where he made fast and we pulled ourselves up, carrying the end of the tow line of the next boat, which carried the next line and so on until the six boats were up. Half a mile further on we came to a place where it was impossible to proceed on this side of the river, there being no place for the men to stand and pull, the water made a kind of a fall, and it was altogether a singular place. We had to try the other side of the river. In crossing we met with many rocks and one island which offered so many favorable eddies, that we rather gained than lost ground. The river here is about three-quarters of a mile wide. On the west shore we found good tracking for about a quarter of a mile, when again the services of our swimmer were required. Finding ourselves on an island, Colonel Alleyne being an experienced boatman said we had done enough for that day and we camped.

On Tuesday, November 4th, we started again with sails and oars. The river being full of islands we had not the same difficulty as the day before, and we reached Sarkametto about 10 a. m, well pleased to find ourselves at the head of these last four cataracts and congratulated ourselves on having brought the first six boats of the Expedition so far.

Next morning I received orders to go down with four boats, which order rather disappointed me, as I had expected to go through to Dongola. I found out that our trip was a trial only. I took all hands into the four boats, the officers also coming aboard, and left at 9 a. m.

Now came the tug of war, the shooting of all the cataracts. Coming up we used all eddies, now we had to avoid them, coming up also if unable to proceed we could draw back and try another channel, now, everything depended on quick judgment and prompt action, the more so as keel boats are not considered fit for rapid work. I ordered my captains to follow at such distances as to give them time to avoid following should the leading boat err in the choice of channel. After shooting the Dal cataract all safe I asked my captains how the boats behaved. All agreed that they were slow in answering their helm and required close watching. Travelling between the cataracts against a strong headwind was slow work and we longed for the next one to get along faster. Shooting the Dal, there had been much dodging of rocks and islands, which gave some excitement. In Akaska cataract we discovered a smooth, straight channel in the middle of the river and not very long.

This shooting of the rapids was a surprise to the Egyptian soldiers, a number of whom were stationed at every cataract. The natives came rushing out of their huts with their children, goats and dogs and stood on the beach to see the North American Indian boatmen. I had more leisure now to look round. I have not seen the place yet where I would care to settle down.

The next cataract is Tangur, which I considered the most dangerous of all for shooting. The river is wide and there are many islands and rocks, the rocks are high, and there are many channels to choose from, and as I had noticed coming up, many of these channels are too crooked for shooting especially with a keel boat, all of which makes this rapid, a dangerous one to shoot. The rocks hide each other and if you clear the first one you find yourself close on the other. A narrow escape I had on the east side of Tangur island. The boat following me had taken a sheer and was obliged to take another channel, which having a swifter current than the one I had taken, brought this boat up with me below the rock so close as nearly to cause a disaster.

Colonel Alleyne ordered lunch near the place, where the steamer Gizeh was wrecked. We could see her high and dry on the rock, where she had laid some time as I was told. After lunch we started for Ambigol cataract. On our way we met several large nuggars with their peculiar sails, going at good speed. These nuggers never track but go up with a strong breeze. We shot Ambigol cataract between three and four o'clock and met five whalers at the foot of it. Colonel Alleyne ordered me to go ashore to speak to them. They were manned by Royal Engineers with foreman Graham and his voyageurs. We started again downwards and made Semnah cataract after sunset shortly before dark. Shooting Semnah gate, finished our day's work and we camped. We had made this day 61 miles.

Dal cataract	5 miles.
From the foot of Dal to the head of Akaska	9 " "
Akaska cataract	1 "
From the foot of Akaska to Tangur	14 "
Tangur cataract	3 "
From the foot of Tangur to Ambigol	9 "
Ambigol cataract	1 "
From the foot of Ambigol to Semneh	17 "
Semneh cataract	2 "
	61 "

This day's experience decided my opinion about the boats. Many of my men had been portaging on the Ottawa for different lumber firms and all agreed with me, that whilst the Nile river boats would have been of no use on the Ottawa, they could not be improved upon for the Nile service on account of the nature of the river. For the ascents of the river as well as the cataracts, the sailing qualities of the boats were all important, and when towed by line the keel would give a chance to shoot out into the current to get round rocks, where a flat bottom would have followed the line broadside and fetched up against the rock. In shooting the cataracts the boats did not answer the helm as quickly as would flat bottoms, but this drawback was not sufficient to condemn the keel.

Next day, Thursday, November 6th, we ran some more swift water to Sarras, nine miles below foot of Semnah. We met there thirty whalers with troops and stores ready to ascend. Colonel Denison asked me to give him one man to act as pilot, so I gave him Mathias Hill, an Iroquois. Colonel Denison went up with this fleet.

Most of the Canadian voyageurs asked me how I found the Rapids. I told them that I had no trouble, considering it unadvisable to give a minute description, as I had already discovered how the fast falling water daily changed the appearance of the river, and what was a good place for me to go up, would be bad now, whilst a bad place might be better. I was well aware that these voyageurs would have more trouble than I had. They had not only larger loads but soldier crews, whilst I had my Caughnawaga boys with whom I had worked from youth up and who promptly caught at a sign from me, while the soldiers had to be talked to, and, although having the best of will, could not always comprehend the situation.

After thirty whalers had started, I was informed by Lord Avonmore of the order to camp. Next day the 7th November, another fleet of twenty-eight boats started. for which Lord Avonmore asked me a pilot. I gave him John Bruce of St. Regis.

The following day, the 8th, Lord Avonmore requested of me seven men and a foreman, to go with him up to the Dal cataract to be stationed there, owing probably, as I thought to myself, that Col. Alleyne considered the Dal the most difficult. I pointed out Peter Canoe as the most experienced boatman I had, and as he does not speak English, James Deer went as their interpreter. I received orders for myself to go down with the rest of my men to Gemai. At Gemai I found twenty-three light boats manned by Dongolese. Placing a captain in each boat we started, but were disappointed to find that these men had never seen a boat nor used an oar. With the help of the usual north wind we managed to ascend in good time to Sarras. On the way up we had to teach one man to steer and then go round to each man and teach him to row. Neither understanding one word of the other's language this was a terrible task. I had however, been long enough in contact with English military discipline by this time, to know that there was no backing out. We loaded at Sarras and proceeded up with Lieut. C. R. Orde as Commander of this convoy, who had an interpreter with him. Without the latter it would have been impossible to get along; as it was, some accidents could not be avoided. Our new commander being an experienced boatman as well as a good carpenter, and a gentleman we managed to keep up with the other fleets. To give an idea of the trouble we had, I need only say that these Dongolese generally understood just the contrary of what they were ordered to do. They would pull hard when asked to stop or stop pulling at some critical place when hard pulling was required. Lieut. Orde as well as myself were continually patching boats on account of these fellows. We made the nine miles from Sarras to Semnah in just six days, whereas we had travelled before at the rate of seventy miles in five days. At Semnah Lieut. Orde reported to Commander Hammill, R. N., in charge of Semnah cataract, Commander Hammill informed me that my plan of ascending Semnah gate was adopted by all the others, he also asked me if I thought I should be able to make boatmen of the Dongolese, I told him I was discouraged and the only consolation I had was that my Dongolese convoy was still travelling as fast as the other fleets in spite of my strict orders always to give the right of way to boats manned by soldiers and to avoid retarding them in the cataracts.

Reaching Ambigol November 19th, during this day I was requested to assist in pulling off a steam pinnace which had run on the rocks and filled, blocking the small channel for steamers to ascend. I having 175 Dongolese with my Caughnawaga boys and about 200 Egyptian soldiers they parted the hawser on the first pull, while getting another hawser Col. Butler arrived in a whaler from Sarras with a crew of Kroomen, with Chief Prince of Manitoba as captain. Col. Butler ordered us to abandon the wreck and explore another channel on the opposite side of the river, I unloaded my boat manned by Caughnawagas and with Lieut. Orde, went across, after half a day's search found a very crooked channel which afterwards 4 or 5 steamers ascended succesfully.

At Tangur it was found advisable to split the convoy, Major Crofton taking 10 boats and Lieut. Orde the rest. Going up some minor cataract with eight Dongolese on the line, and one young fellow, a little brighter than the rest, in the boat with me and having just passed the worst place, a couple of the men ashore got to fighting and the rest let go the line either to part them or to join and I was left at the mercy of the rapid for a variety. These men were, as I said before, entirely unused to boats. They are all excellent swimmers and able to cross the river at almost any place. When making long distances they make use of the goat skin bottles they have for carrying water, scolding was of no use, they neither understood nor cared. I may here mention another peculiarity of theirs. I had noticed many scars on their bodies, but could not account for it, until one of them fell sick when the other cut his skin to bleed him, and filled the cut with sand.

This convoy carried about sixty tons of freight, all of which was brought safely to the foot of Dal cataract and the convoy was ordered downwards again as far as the head of Ambigol cataract for reloading. As I could not trust the Dongolese in shooting the rapids I manned the boats with my Iroquois and made trips at each cataract, letting the Dongolese walk. It was a grand sight to see so many boats on their way up, some sailing, some rowing, some tracking and some on shore patching up.

We reached the head of Ambigol, loaded up and started up stream. We made the foot of Dal with less trouble on this trip, the Dongolese having learned a great deal as well as I and my men knowing now some words of their language.

On arriving at Dal, I found that this place had become a very busy scene. Many tents were pitched among which were a commissariat, a post office and a number of officers tents. Lord Avonmore had come down from the middle of the Dal cataract, next to his tent was that of Colonel Burnaby, then Major Mann, near the beach was Sir George Arthur, who had arrived that day from below, commanding a convoy of boats. On the south end of the little colony were Lord Charles Beresford, Col. Alleyne and Major Spaight. Col. Alleyne congratulated me on my success with the Dongolese.

I returned for another trip, arriving back here on the 19th of December. The same officers were still here. The next morning Col. Alleyne ordered me to camp on the beach with my men and said we had had done enough of lower cataract service. At the same time the Dongolese, that had been with me still in charge of Major Crofton, were sent down to try a trip by themselves. It proved lucky for these men that the Nile does not scare them, for they had to swim for it on more than one occasion. However, they proved efficient in the end to the satisfaction of the officers.

While lying on my oars I had an opportunity to admire the passing army, both officers and men, and their discipline. I did not see one private soldier who looked more than thirty years of age. The soldiers showed signs of the hard work they had done in getting up the Nile. Their hands were blistered and their clothes worn out, but they were as

cheerful and enthusiastic as ever. My orders now were
to assist the officer in charge with my Iroquois in
passing boats up the Dal cataract, until the last boat
was passed. I had all my men collected here except
four who were stationed above. During this time I
saw Colonel Burnaby depart on his camels, Lord
Avonmore in his boat, my old commander Col. Alleyne
in his boat and afterwards Sir Evelyn Wood on horse-
back, also our Canadian officer Col. Kennedy, Surgeon,
Major Neilson, and Col. Grove. The river had now
fallen so much that there were hundreds of rocks in
sight, in front of this station, and crocodiles could be
seen by the dozen, sunning themselves on the rocks,
Major Mann and Abbe Bouchard with the help of a
powerful glass, pronounced one brute to be twenty-
five feet long.

The last boat that I assisted in passing was on the
14th of January and on the 15th I received orders to
start for Wady Halfa, which brought my active service in the Egyptian Expedition to a close.

We arrived at Wady Halfa on the 18th of January
where I found Captains Aumond and McRae and nearly
two hundred voyageurs. At Wady Halfa I witnessed
the military funeral of a Gordon Highlander, which
was a novel sight to me.

One dark night, long after the retiring bugle had
sounded, an alarm gun was fired. I went out of my
tent and to my astonishment I found the soldiers already prepared to fight. No lights had been used and it
was a mystery to me how the men could get ready in so
short a time. I could see that in a real attack, the
enemy would not get much advantage over these men.

I must mention here a curious sight I witnessed at
the funeral of an Egyptian, before lowering the body
into the grave they put a small coin into his mouth,
and I found out, that their belief is, that the dead
have to cross a river to get into the " happy hunting
grounds" and I concluded that the ferryman, not ferry-
ing on " tick " they had provided their comrade with
his fare. Before leaving Wady Halfa, I had the
satisfaction to see two of my Iroquois carry off the
first prizes for running at the United Service Sports,
held under the patronage of the Station Commandant
Col. Duncan and the officers.

We left Wady Halfa on the 29th January, arriving
at Cairo, February 5th, where an opportunity was
given us to visit the following places of interest :
Kass el-Nil Bridge, Kass-el-Nil Barracks, Abdin Square
and Palace, The Mosque Sultan-Hassan, the Citadel,
the Mosque Mohamet-Ali, the Native Bazaar, the
Esbediah Gardens, and finally Gizeh and the Pyramids.

We sailed from Alexandria on February 6th, 1885,
well pleased with what we had seen in the land of the
Pharos and proud to have shown the world that the
dwellers on the banks of the Nile, after navigating it
for centuries, could still learn something of the craft
from the Iroquois Indians of North America and the
Canadian voyageurs of many races.

I cannot conclude without expressing my satisfaction at the handsome treatment accorded us by the
British Government, and should our services be of
assistance in the proposed Fall campaign in Egypt,
they will be freely given. We were allowed just double
the amount of clothing stipulated in the contract, the

overcoats being given to us at Malta on our way home.

Judging by the stores we conveyed up the Nile the army will not fare badly, we carried Armour's beef, bacon, preserved meat, mutton, vegetables, Ebswurt's crushed peas for soup, pickles, pepper, salt, vinegar, hard biscuit, cabin biscuit, flour, oatmeal, rice, sugar, tea, coffee, cheese, jam, medicine, lime juice, soap, matches, tobacco.

Whoever designed the boats struck the right dimensions perfectly. Each boat was made to carry ten days' rations, including everything in the above list, for a hundred men, ten men with kits and accoutrements, and about a half ton of ammunition.

FINIS.

www.ingramcontent.com/pod-product-compliance
Lightning Source LLC
Chambersburg PA
CBHW032138080426
42733CB00008B/1124